Adventure into Transformation

By the same author
The World Beyond Today
Ancient Memories, New Beginnings

Adventure into Transformation

A Guide to Your New Existence

Merriene Scott

with her spiritual messengers
from Illanitis

Published by Merriene Scott
Email: merriene@merrienescott.com

First Edition published 2003
Second Edition published 2014
Third Edition published 2019
Adventure into Transformation is the second book of a trilogy,
'Messages from Illanitis'.

National Library of Australia
Cataloguing-in-Publication entry

Scott, Merriene.
Adventure into transformation:
a guide to your new existence.

ISBN 978-0-9751058-6-3
eBook: 978-0-9751058-9-4
1. Spiritualism. 2. Self-actualisation (Psychology).
I. Title.
133.93

Typeset in 13/19 Bembo by Perth Editorial Service
Printed by Iprintplus, Perth
Cover image by Jamie Scott (www.jamiescottimages.com)

All the world's a stage,
and all the men and women merely players.
Shakespeare As You Like It

Contents

Acknowledgments

The journey of writing this book has been made so much easier and much more enjoyable through the most wonderful assistance of my friend Irene Percy, who transferred all of my freehand writing so ably onto the computer and thus transformed all the messages into readable print.

Grateful thanks also to Dr Janet Wale for initial editing. To Allan Watson, my deep appreciation and gratitude for your caring and respectful final editing along with your wonderful support and friendship. My loving wishes to all the agents of assistance – family, friends and colleagues – who have been there at the perfect moments to encourage me to publish this second book in the trilogy.

About the Front Cover

The beautiful photograph of the passionfruit flower
was taken by my son Jamie Scott. It symbolises the
magic of creation – the beauty of sacred geometry –
and offers the invitation to live with true passion
and so bring about a transformation into
authenticity of being.
My loving thanks, Jamie.

Preface

Adventure into Transformation is the second book of a trilogy, 'Messages from Illanitis'.

Through automatic writing from a loving source of wisdom and knowing, I have transcribed messages for you to ponder on and perhaps identify with as your own truth of understanding. It has been a privilege once again to have received this information.

As in the first book, *The World Beyond Today*, the sometimes quaint sentence structures have been left in their original form to retain the rhythm and metre, which embody a divine coding assisting you to receive the intent of the words on all levels of your being.

I suggest reading this book in a quiet place will help you to gain full benefit from its contents.

Joy, love and blessings.

Merriene Scott

Introduction

The beginning of your New World is coming very rapidly and, as you dear reader are aware, your time as a three-dimensional human being is changing to a new way of existing. We are in your reality to show you the way forward into this different way of existing in a multidimensional form. As you read on, many fresh possibilities will be explained to you. We are messengers from Illanitis, forever present with Merriene to help her assist you, as mankind, to understand your coming reality with love and joy as well as with fun and compassion for all you are connected to.

Our role in your reality is one of creating experiences for you to learn these new ways and to be continuously comfortable in the multidimensional state. Perhaps you are aware of your abilities to teleport and to manifest whatever you desire very easily, and yet to live in a state of detachment from material wants and needs. We believe many of you are very ready for further understanding of where you are now going with your changing state of existence – into a world of thoughtfulness and lightness. We explain to you the very best choices you can make to utilise your abilities and to assist the human race in evolution to a different species as such.

This little book presents a different mode of assistance on every second page, and as you read through the pages you will gain insight into your reason for being and the very nature of your existence at this point of space and time. We consider that many of you understand the need to love yourself and to love your fellow man, unconditionally. As you develop great trust in the ways of Spirit, you will find the suggestions contained on the following pages very valid and necessary in all the steps you are taking on your path to enlightenment. Perhaps your progress has been slow and laborious. Perhaps you have not seen the light glowing ahead of you to show you the way, and at times your trust has been very shaky. We know being human is a very courageous experience, and, as we wish you to fulfill your reasons for coming to the Earth plane, we lift you up and carry you forward along your spiritual path.

The way is always full of hazards and detours that slow you down. With knowledge and wisdom you can bypass these detours and deal with the hazards with amazing ease. The following pages give you the skills and tools to proceed with joy and anticipation.

We have the ability to be with each of you as you ponder over these ideas. We assist each of you individually to bring your transformation further into the light of love. You will feel a great connection with your own God/Goddess within and live with your own great truth shining brightly, your way of living transformed. You will never again feel alone or lost in your quest for understanding or your reason for being. The comfort of knowing you are full of the Divine Presence and are surrounded with the loving energy of all existence will help you to come into your own power. The power you have is unique to you and, as each of you connects your energy to the power of universal wisdom, the whole of mankind will transform to a beautiful collection of love energies.

With the beginning of your new existence coming very rapidly, we are eager for you to be ready on all levels of your being for transformation into a lighter being of loving energy, letting go your old ways of being and doing. By this we mean you will have no need to work as you do, struggling to live in the material and physical ways you have been doing for so many centuries. This way of existence is now trans- forming, with you all being restructured to another way of looking and being internally.

As you may well know, your vibrations have been changing in the last few years, and many of you have found your ability to communicate with Spirit and to live multidimensionally. This is your future way of being, and, as your vibrations stabilise at a higher frequency, you will no longer live only in the physical world. We are so very happy that your awareness of these changes is now apparent, allowing you to transform quickly amidst the growing chaos. There is no need to remain around the pain and suffering that will surely occur to those who remain with the lower vibrations. We wish you to think deeply around the question we are asking: How do you think and feel about yourself and why are you on the Earth plane? The following pages will give you some answers to this question and, as you read, you will absorb into your psyche the very best reasons for being. You will be given guidelines to help you change your thinking and feelings. These instructions will be to your soul and not your ego personality. Your soul already knows the answers as to why you are on the planet;

it is your personality as you have chosen it to be at this time that does not readily accept the advice or wisdom given.

Allow yourself to recognise your soul and its ability to remember this information. Once you give permission to allow the information to be given attention and respect, you will be very successful on your path to transformation. It is very important to trust and respect the words that you read; please ponder on each page for a while before moving on to the next.

Remember we are working with you as you read the words, on other levels of your being. As you allow yourself to receive these messages from Spirit, you will truly become one with the God/Goddess within you. We can heal you and move you forward in your evolution very quickly as you accept your reason for being. Please remember this. And as you take in the following wisdom, your transformation to a being of light and understanding will occur.

Your next goal is to live authentically, with a knowingness of your very own power, thereby assisting in the transformation of this planet to one of infinite joy, beauty and love, as you also will be doing. When your joy is complete, you will have the satisfaction of knowing you are living as you are truly meant to.

Part One

Wisdom

Men and women have wisdom when their level of awareness is high and their understanding of the broader concept of existence is developed. With this awareness and understanding comes the knowing that everything in existence is exactly as it is meant to be. There is no need to struggle, worry or create effort in what you do. Wisdom of knowing you are one with all there is assists you in your choices in the three-dimensional world.

As you come into your own wise knowingness, you become humble and gracious to those who are not yet ready to discover the secret of wisdom. One cannot give another wisdom. It just is, and each of you arrives at this state in your own way and time. The coming of wisdom is earned, usually through many experiences during many lifetimes.

Your memory retains your understanding of each experience you have ever had. The nature of you is the culmination of all these experiences and all the choices you have made in regard to these experiences. You all have had much suffering and joy in many lifetimes. Perhaps, having lived as both a pauper and a king, you have had a knowing of both. These memories are stored deep within your cells, and in this lifetime you will act and react in certain ways using these memories, unrecognised by you consciously, to resolve a situation you are in.

With awareness and understanding you can change your actions or build on them, creating a wonderful source of power within. Please acknowledge your wisdom of thought and action, and know this is your soul – your intuition and your heart – that speaks. Much knowledge is already available for you in your libraries within.

Meditation

Transformation will be so very easy for you, dear reader, when you give yourself time to sit and go to the real you within. You can reach in during meditation and listen to your heart. Your heart is representative of your pure soul and, as you listen to this wonderful part of you, answers will be there for you. Meditation allows you to turn to your soul's messages as you give attention and respect to what lies within this purest part of you.

By sitting in the silence, or walking in nature, you are connecting with your God/Goddess and the Creator of all there is. You are the master/mistress of your own destiny, and when you listen to your heart you will remember who you truly are and why you are here at this time of great change.

Meditation takes you back to the authentic soul you truly are, the soul who has lived many, many lives and has experienced much in the way of hardships and pleasures. The culmination of all these experiences resides in your soul, and, as you listen to your heart telling you of your wisdom, you will find your decision-making processes easy and joyful.

Intuition

Most humans operate their lives using the five senses: hearing, seeing, touching, tasting and smelling. Very few use their sixth sense – the feeling of the heart – which can be called intuition or intuitive thought. Yet the very best way to live is with listening to, or feeling, the messages of the heart. As you do, and as you act on the messages given, you will find you have greater success in all you do. These messages are usually the very first feelings you have when faced with a situation or a person and you need to decide what course of action to take. By listening to your intuition you will make the correct choice, even if the choice seems wrong in the short term. You will find, as time goes on, you are right in the decision you have made.

Every one of you can receive messages from Spirit in this way. We encourage you to trust what you feel or hear in your heart. The heart is the soul, and your soul has the wisdom of all lifetimes held within. By listening to your soul, you will receive clear messages to assist you with your purpose here, in this lifetime. Meditation assists you to open up your intuitive thought, although not always immediately at the time of meditation. This time set aside opens you to communication with your soul by showing you how to still your mind and listen to your heart instead. As you still your mind, you also still your ego personality and begin to develop a relationship with the real you residing within.

Intuition is the bridging sense between your physical reality and your spiritual reality. When you have developed your intuition, and trust the messages you receive, you are well prepared for further opening to your multidimensional faculties.

Trust

Trusting in yourself as a wise and beautiful soul is very important in your transformation. As you learn to trust that the circumstances you are in are your choice, and as you trust your power within to create the future you desire, you will find you can create whatever opportunities you wish for yourself.

Trust in loving all unconditionally, and that includes yourself. Trust you are protected from harm, trust your connection to universal wisdom and trust that the God/Goddess is ever powerful and loving.

Remember the trust you have needs to come from your heart and intuitive feeling and not be the trust you may call reason from your mind thoughts. That reasoning from the ego/personality source can easily sway your actions and decisions.

As you open up to complete trust in your connection to the divine within yourself, miracles begin to occur in your life. As they do, you will be continually blessed and encouraged in your quest for enlightenment.

Your positive energies allow Spirit to access your soul rapidly and continuously, giving you radiance and also confirmation of your courageous decision to walk the path of a loving new existence.

Going to Your
God/Goddess Within

Throughout time, humans have considered God as a separate entity who presides over mankind with an allpowerful energy and who must be feared and obeyed. As you become spiritually more awake and aware, you realise that there is no entity in the heavens keeping a check on your life. To consider that one is at the mercy of God, in heaven or in hell, is an extremely inappropriate concept, and has created the opportunity for churches to control vast numbers of people with their dogmas and doctrines. Many of you are now coming to the understanding of God/Goddess as lovingly present everywhere.

We use the word God with the understanding that both masculine and feminine energies are contained within it; and, by stating that God is everywhere, we mean that He/She is the very core of every living cell and is all-encompassing in every atom or particle of existence. A bird possesses its very own God, as do you and as does every plant and every grain of sand.

God within is all there is, and is the very purest part of our knowing, coming from love and not fear. Your pure knowing is linked to the universal source of all creation, and with this linking you are connected to every other existing being and thing. We are all one and from the same source. You have taken on an identity as a human, with a human personality, to create your unique individuality for the purpose you are here. We are all playing different roles, continuing the work of the universe as one. You are so very important, in your individual role, in your purpose for being. It is very important for you to visit and communicate with your God within continuously, maintaining your connection with your true source and knowing.

This is your truth – your very own God is the only God you need. Other outside 'Gods' are not necessary for your purpose. The God within each and every one of you is the very core of your being, and as you listen you will have clarity, joy and success in all you do.

Being Passionate about
Your Own Truth

You have your very own truth that is unique to you and you alone. When you find your truth, you will realise that you have found the reason why you are in human, physical existence. Understanding this, you live with passion for your own truth and with a zest for living. Your passion is your truth, and, when you sit in the silence listening to your heart's desire, you will recognise your special times when you are at your happiest and feel most fulfilled.

As you live your passion, you are also living in your truth. You become who you truly are. Being your authentic self, you can succeed in every area of your life.

Being passionate, you are aligning your vibrations into perfect harmony with universal truth and allowing the opening of your heart into greater graciousness with all there is. This harmony allows you to resonate in perfect rhythm with existence, creating a blending of loving energies and enabling you to work and play at your highest level of wisdom.

As you discover your truth, please look at it closely and allow time to absorb your feelings. Do not compare yourself with others, as you are you and your role is unique to you.

We can assist you as you learn to be courageous and speak your truth. When you do, you will attract to you those who are to learn with you of their truth that may still be hidden.

The Meaning of Truth

What is meant by this word truth? We have been telling you to live your very own truth, so now we will explain to you our definition of this word and what it represents. The word truth is a lovely way of saying 'being at one with God'. When you and your own God/ Goddess are in perfect harmony, being as one, you are in truth, you are the representative of God you are meant to be. This blending of your soul with the source of all creation in perfect oneness and bliss is your truth of beingness. Please understand you are unique in the way you will blend with God. You are living as a representative of the Creator and you can trust that you are as you are meant to be.

With trust in and love of who you truly are, you are living your truth. You have no need to compare yourself with anyone else. When you stand as an individual with honour and respect for yourself in all your own power and glory, then you can say to yourself that you are living your truth.

The nature of your being is excited and supportive as your personality comes to the realisation of who you truly are. As you – your personality – begin to merge with your soul self, who has always known your truth as a perfect, beautiful being, the old patterns of justifying your thoughts and feelings to others leave you. You feel so very happy and confident, speaking and living your truth as you know it to be.

Truth is the key to your own power within. Please honour it and live joyously and consistently in relationship both with yourself and with others.

The Beginning of
the New You

With increased awareness, you change in your thinking and feelings about yourself, yet something is pulling you. You are aware of your current habits and patterns for coping with each day. Perhaps you like the old you, and are very comfortable in the way you have been living your life. Habits are unconscious ways of doing and being, and do not create new thoughts, ideas or ways of being, so that much of the day goes by in the same way it has done for a long while.

Please begin to open up to new ways of doing the same repetitive things. Perhaps this could be, for example, in showering or bathing. Use your creative thinking in honouring your physical body that you are about to clean. Actually talk to your body as you prepare to wash and thank it for being your vehicle. Ask it what changes it might like in the way you nourish it externally, also how to exercise it more effectively, what areas of it feel neglected and need special attention.

We consider that by talking to all parts of your body externally and internally and asking for messages in response, you will know which areas to focus on and can restore harmony to this wonderful person called you.

Bodies come in all shapes and sizes, with many reasons for their being so. Your body is your temple for your soul, and, as you understand this and begin to honour it, it can change to a very beautiful reflection of you as an enlightened being, with your wisdom and joy reflecting through each part of it. Illnesses will not be a problem with you, as you will be at such ease with yourself. Illness only comes to those who have dis-ease. Remember, the you of now is a very powerful being.

The more you are aware of this, the more success you will have in all you do as you set about achieving your purpose here in this lifetime.

Changes to Your Body

The changes to your body are most evident to you as you become more of who you truly are and connect more strongly with your God/ Goddess within. As you notice these changes, you see confirmation of becoming one with God and living truly in the light of your own truth. Your body will glow and radiate your love and beauty of thought and feelings. To others you will look serene, joyful and balanced. The very nature of you will be relaxed and wise, forever exuding a feeling of peace and comfort to those around you, which will assist them in seeking a similar position.

The explanation for these changes in your physicality is that your chakras (energy centres within the body) are totally in harmony and connecting with the etheric part of your being at all points equally, bringing into play the strong connection between your physical and subtle bodies. The nature of you is beautifully and perfectly intertwined between your non-physical (subtle) and physical bodies, and so you can operate fully in all dimensions of your being.

Until you as a human have arrived at this awareness and understanding, your physical bodies and subtle bodies are quite distorted and are not intertwined as such. So many humans do not live fully as spiritual beings in a physical body.

The perfect blending of your subtle and physical bodies brings you to a new state of being, and as you do so you will find you have excellent health and wellbeing in your thoughts, feelings and actions. There will be perfect flow between all your chakras, allowing you to live fully as a vital and loving being.

The Way to Eat

As you become more spiritually aware, your body needs different fuels for nourishment. The structure of your body is altering as the cells begin to vibrate at a higher frequency. This will allow you to function so much more easily and with greater flow. Energy\will be utilised more efficiently as you are in harmony with yourself.

As this change occurs, your eating requirements alter. You will discover you do not have an appetite for meat or other animal products. You will be drawn toward eating only the freshest, purest fruit and vegetables, and you will enjoy eating them in their natural state of wholeness, as nature intended them to be eaten. As your awareness grows, you will begin to see the benefits of the best ways of nourishing yourself. Your body will feel light and fluid, without the heaviness you possibly have experienced many a time before when you indulged in so-called lovely hot dinners.

The desire for this change in eating will come as your need for emotional comfort from the food you eat diminishes. Food is a source of energy for your body, so as you learn to receive and exchange energy easily, with love and awareness, food will lose its importance to you. The sun is the greatest source of energy, and your ability to receive nourishment directly from this source will be all you need one day.

In the meantime, please understand that fresh, raw fruit, vegetables, nuts and seeds, along with pure spring water, are the very best choices you can make for fuel. They allow your vehicle to house you as a personality and soul for the length of linear time necessary for the purpose you are here for now.

Understanding

Understanding the ways of Spirit is very important in your new way of being. Not understanding the nature of your existence as you are would hinder your progress, so we wish to explain to you your nature as a spiritual being having a human experience, first and foremost. You are spirit in a physical form to enable you to have experiences of many kinds that are not possible in spirit. You needed to manifest a human body to have physical experiences, and, as you created your existence in the physical plane, you chose experiences and lessons to assist you to learn to have great understanding of yourself as a soul connected to all that there is in existence.

Please understand you are the director and actor in your play of life. You have taken on a personality that will create the circumstances in your play to have the experience of love, anger, betrayal, humility and many other emotional conditions.

The others in your play are also actors playing out the roles assigned to them. They are assisting you to learn from every encounter or experience as it occurs. As you begin to understand this, you will remain detached from the issues at hand and move on effortlessly in the acts of your play of life.

Connecting with Spirit

You are not alone as you act out your role in this lifetime. You have your backstage crew, so to speak, assisting you whenever you are in need. This backstage crew is your spiritual helpers, whether they are your own personal guides, angels or others from afar as we are. Your helpers have been assigned to their particular roles also, in your play. They are not in physical form, so they cannot be seen, just as backstage members of a production are not visible to the players or the audience. Most humans have forgotten that they have their helpers behind the scenes, and do not consult with them as they direct and act out their play. The helpers are still there assisting as they can, so that the play goes as planned. The moment you, the actor, realise that you have this assistance behind the scenes is a moment of great celebration for all of us in spirit.

We can have more cooperation and understanding from you in the physical when you are aware of us. As this awareness of our presence grows, we can connect with you more effectively, and communication can become a two-way channel for greater understanding and achievement in all you need to do. Your play will become the success it is meant to be.

Dialogue with Spirit

The time is here now for you to have greater dialogue with Spirit, as you open up your channels to higher vibrations. We are encouraging this profusion of exchange to effect more understanding and for you to define your role more clearly.

As the world becomes more chaotic, an ability to understand why will assist you to prepare for a new/ renewed existence as a being with greater transparency. You will communicate with us very easily, in the way most suited to you. You are all capable of this in one or more ways, be it by seeing, hearing, feeling or knowing; and, as you trust your messages in whatever way they come, you will receive them more often and more clearly.

Please ask only for the messages from God – Prime Source, Creator or Highest Knowing (what feels comfortable for you) – and your highest guidance. You will be able to have a direct link with the God/ Goddess who resides within all. Your guides or helpers are messengers of God and will give you the messages necessary for your highest good and purpose. The messages you receive will be profound in their meaning for you, and the instructions given will be for you alone, and not for others.

You have your own particular truth and you have a special role now in the transformation of the human race. Listen graciously to your messages and, as you do, take action accordingly. Remember that your role as a divine being is foremost in your play at this time.

Understanding Your
Messages from Spirit

As you become more aware of who you truly are, you begin to live more fully as a spiritual being with a knowing that you are playing a role as a physical human. As you become more aware of your knowing, your ability to communicate with those assisting you will become easier. Sometimes this communication is with that other part of you known as your higher self or super-consciousness, which contains the wisdom of the universal consciousness we call God. Your ability to communicate with energies from beyond this sphere will become available to you as you trust and love yourself unconditionally. You give yourself over to living in a state of surrender to sources of wisdom that are available to our collective consciousness.

We can explain this to you as wisdom from the angelic realms and from other forms of intelligence. As long as you are living with truthful intent, great integrity and humility, these sources of information and knowledge are available to you. You have available the best possible guidance to assist you in your transformation to higher frequencies of existence.

As we have mentioned earlier, you have unique ways of connecting and communicating with Spirit. Some of you will find it easy to see visions and understand your messages this way. Others will hear messages in your thoughts or feel them in your heart. Some of you will find you are saying words of great wisdom to others when you have no idea how you knew the information or had the knowledge. Others of you may be inspired to write, and will find words flow from your pen as you sit in the silence.

Whichever way you receive your messages, understand we are very grateful for your willingness to listen and acknowledge our existence in your lives. Only then can we assist you to reach your fullest potential. As that happens, you reach fulfillment in your once forgotten, and now remembered, agendas for this lifetime.

Opening to Receive Messages Clearly

Receiving messages from Spirit is a wonderful experience for you. As you trust the process, you will have the willingness to act on what is suggested for you to do and to be. Many of you may not, however, fully prepare yourselves to receive only the purest and wisest advice available, and we now wish to share with you the way toward only allowing in the very best messages.

Firstly, we suggest you sit very quietly and ask only for your very highest guidance, giving you messages with the very purest advice for your highest good.

You can ask for this verbally no matter which way you receive your messages, and perhaps, if it fits comfortably with you, you can ask in the name of God/Goddess. When you have received your messages, we also suggest you give gratitude for the advice given. That will be greatly appreciated by your spiritual assistants.

A second important undertaking, especially in the early stages of your communication with Spirit, is the clearing and opening of your channel connecting you to Spirit. This is via a chakra or energy centre called the Causal chakra, at the back of your head. When you first begin to communicate, this opening will be small, so we encourage you to think of it becoming wide and clear. You can visualise this or you can feel it doing so in your thoughts. The intention will then be there, and this is enough for this chakra to open and receive more effectively.

Another lovely way to open up all your body energy centres so they are in perfect harmony is by spinning yourself clockwise and anticlockwise. Not only does this bring your body into beautiful balance, it releases any tensions that may be there to block messages.

Being a Beacon of Light
for Others

As your awareness grows of yourself as a beautiful loving energy, you come to the understanding that we are all one. By this we mean that all of mankind comes from the Creator of all things; you are not separate from God, you are part of God. To explain it another way, we all have God within us, and as you become aware of this you connect more strongly with the inner part of you. Your energy frequency will change, and heaviness of form and thinking will leave you.

You will have a lightness of feeling, thinking and being. You will glow with a beacon of 'light', as your aura – the energy field surrounding you – will be radiantly beautiful and full of loving energy. It will magnetically attract many people who need to be shown the way forward along their paths. You will lose your density, allowing you to live more in other dimensions of yourself more often.

As this occurs, your ability to help others will accelerate in many ways. Perhaps the words you speak will be thoughtful and loving, and your life will flow with great harmony for others to see and begin to wonder why. Your attitude to your so-called problems will be full of loving, insightful wisdom, and, when these problems are resolved swiftly and with grace, others will notice.

Your beacon of light shines forth for you to show others the way. You can only do so by example. As you do, you bring completion of your service to others – not by doing for them, but by showing them how to do it. Life is easy and exhilarating for those of you who become aware of your true nature and detach yourselves from worry about or fear of the problems of life. Remember you are in a play, and you are director/ actor of this play. Your real self is a pure, loving being of light. The light of God is within you.

Forgiveness

Forgiveness is the ability to let go of hurts from actions by others who were part of your past experiences and learning. As you forgive these people, you free yourself to live in the present moment without hanging on to your wounds within. Forgiveness of past actions and release of the memories retained are necessary for your spiritual growth to progress easily.

Those who do not forgive create blocks to future growth and the opportunities that may occur for them. The action of forgiveness frees you from the bondage you still have with the persons concerned. The energy between you will flow freely once again as you remove the barrier caused by the reluctance to let go of these past deeds. Acknowledge to yourself that the hurt caused was your choice, and you have gained useful learning from these hurtful actions and words.

When you look at the situation from a different perspective, you see that your hurts were due to a part of yourself not feeling whole or authentic. This is why you have been affected by the action that was hurtful to you. With many deep thoughts, you can strengthen this vulnerable part of yourself, healing the hurts and letting go of the actions that created the wound within.

In the forgiveness of others we remind you to be very aware of forgiving yourself where necessary for past unkind or unloving deeds you have done to others or yourself. Let go of your guilt or worry and know, in the awareness you now have, the understanding will be there of the lessons learnt and insight gained from your thoughtless actions.

The act of forgiveness shows that your wounds are healed. You are now self-empowered and detached from emotional dramas in your life. You have no need to hold a grudge with anyone or anything, and in this freeing up of yourself you become light – and liberated from the dramas of living in the physical world.

We consider that the act of forgiveness is one of the most uplifting and self-empowering acts of mankind. To forgive is to give your soul freedom to 'fly'.

Discipline

The ability to 'fly' as a human is not as difficult as you may think. You live mostly in a three-dimensional world that has gravity; your physical body is dense and relatively heavy. As you lighten up, however, and move toward other ways of existing, you find you become less dense and move into other dimensions of being, while still also present in the third dimension. You can change your frequency to a faster, higher one that frees you from being bound to the Earth. Then you can 'fly'.

This takes discipline, and the steps toward achieving this wonderful state of being are many. Frequent meditation brings you quickly to these higher frequencies, as do thoughts of love and kindness. Your discipline of self to live authentically with great trust and an awareness and alertness to the oneness of all in existence creates the best possible conditions to enable you to 'fly'.

Discipline is necessary for you to achieve clarity of thought, purpose and vision. Without it, you can be taken off track very easily by temptations presented to you in many forms. Without discipline you would find yourself stuck in three-dimensional reality more often than you would want.

As you progress in your spiritual growth, you discover the joys of choosing your state of being for each occasion, fully aware of your power to do so. Discipline of thought, word and action in every moment strengthens your energy and substance. Eventually you become a loving 'ball' of pureness and light contained within your physical vehicle, with the ability to change form and realities. You move swiftly, not only around the Earth but throughout the cosmos.

Please understand, the discipline we are talking of is self-discipline, with all choices being yours and yours alone. You are then free to be of assistance to many in their understanding of self-discipline.

The Nature of Living Freely

Freedom to be who you truly are is your right. Freedom from the conditioning you received as a child is a major challenge for you as an adult. Freedom to live in the present moment with joy and awareness is your ultimate task. It can be obtained as you acknowledge that your past has brought you the wisdom you now have. As you process and acknowledge your past, you can let it go, knowing that it has served its purpose in bringing you to who you are now.

Are you the person you truly are meant to be? Perhaps you have more work to do to unravel deep hurts and wounds from earlier experiences. This will come to your awareness a little at a time, and only then can it be dealt with – little by little. It is similar to going through a box of memories: those at the top are looked at first and you work your way to the bottom. Only when you have let go of the top memories will the bottom memories be exposed and become available to be dealt with.

Continue from time to time to face and attend to these memories. Deal with them perhaps with the help of a counsellor, then let them go with gratitude and understanding for their place in your growth. Only when you get to the bottom of the box – which also needs discarding – will you have true freedom as a soul contained within your vehicle in this lifetime.

Freedom as a soul still in a physical body gives you the opportunity to live truly as you are meant to do and to be, achieving your purpose here on the Earth plane. With freedom, self-empowerment is complete and you are no longer beholden to anyone or any situation. The opportunities are there for you to bring joy, healing and knowledge to a vast number of people. You feel light, are light and shine a light for all those still in the dark.

Patience

Many of you are very eager to arrive at a state of enlightenment and are anxious to be available to be of service to others. Please be patient and allow the process to occur in its own good time. Patience is a virtue: many hiccups can occur when patience is not adhered to. Rushing to achieve understanding and awareness is not possible, as only when certain experiences have taken place will the circumstances be right for the next step on your path to enlightenment to be lit up for you.

Listen to your heart, knowing your need to wait for situations to come to you and for opportunities to be taken. You know in your deepest part within that you need to be patient, for these times to come. Sometimes situations arise very quickly, before you think you are ready for them, and at other times they arise long after your expectations of them.

You will be happy to understand that for those of you who have asked for a certain person or situation to arise in your lives, it will come. All you need do is put out to the universe your desire and intention, and it will be attended to. Sometimes much learning needs to be accomplished first, before a request can be granted. When a request is for the highest good of the individual, the need will be met.

Patience is difficult for those of you who are very efficient, organised people. As you wait, recognition will come of variants of your request, and your perceptions will change in your waiting.

We challenge you all to listen to your hearts as you develop patience in waiting for your desires to be met. You may discover the delights of the unexpected coming to you, with no effort and no waiting.

Living in the now, the present moment, takes away the need for patience, as your every 'now' is perfect and every future moment will also be perfect, no matter what happens.

Patience of Spirit

Spirit is so very patient with you, as mankind, as you come to the awareness of our presence. We serve you constantly, from birth, with loving care and protection, assisting in your learning, your growing, your experiences and your choices in the decisions you make. As you grow and adopt behaviours to suit your needs and circumstances, the experiences you bring to yourself are those you need for your development on all levels of your being.

Perhaps you have chosen to experience betrayal and denial in this lifetime, in which case you bring into your life those people (actors playing their roles) and circumstances that create the situations needed to experience betrayal and denial. If you do not deal well with these situations, others will arise over and over again, with similar issues, until you deal with and resolve them.

We in Spirit, in all our guises, watch and wait for your growth as a soul. We celebrate each time you pass another level in awareness and understanding. We are very patient, and watch with admiration as you experience living as a human being. We too learn from the vast array of emotions you express, as you experience the many tragedies and joys of living. Many of you have grown in your awareness of our existence in your lives, and our ability to assist you has become much greater so that development comes more rapidly for you.

We have patience with those who are not awakening to the knowledge of our existence in their lives, and continue to guide them with love and understanding. Their position in the scheme of things is valuable and perfect nonetheless, and we ask you who are now awake to respect and love these people without judgment or criticism for their lack of awareness. All are equal in divine law.

Tolerance

To be able to tolerate your fellow man and threedimensional life is an admirable trait. As you awaken to the knowing of who you truly are and why you are on the Earth plane, you begin to see and understand the reasons for differences between each of you and the way you live. The reason for your being is very different from anyone else's, you having your own unique agenda. Only you can follow this, as everyone else has his or her own agenda too. Each and every one of you needs to do things in your own unique way, which may not be understood by others.

With tolerance for other people's different perceptions and modes of living, you can live in harmony with love of all mankind. Do not judge others for their lifestyles or their failure to live up to your expectations. Just move out of their energy space if possible and love them unconditionally. They have chosen to be in the situation that they are for their learning and to experience certain emotions and feelings that are necessary for their evolution.

As you open up your heart to tolerate all manner of ideas, values and types of people, you enrich your soul, discovering the wonderful benefits of allowing others to touch you with their truths and reasons for being.

With tolerance of heart and mind, your progress is rapid – and fun. Your level of understanding for mankind expands with new perceptions of yourself and others.

Having said this, we do not condone tolerance of unacceptable behaviour of any kind. Many use unacceptable behaviour to manipulate and control you and your surroundings. Please see the difference, and, while you stay detached from their behaviour, either remove yourself from the unfavourable energy or remain passive and non-reactionary to it. This will negate the power the person involved is seeking, so that they will cease the behaviour.

Showing Your Truth
to Others

Perhaps by now you are beginning to feel comfortable with the new you, who lives with a very different perspective of who you truly are. As this occurs, you are able to enjoy your three-dimensional (physical) reality without fearing your attachment to any outcomes or happenings in your life. As you let go the fear of or worry about what may happen to you as a result of an issue, you can express joy, living in each moment with intensity and savouring the beauty of all that is occurring. When you allow this to take place, your whole nature is freed so that you are truly living in your authenticity as you, the soul.

Your soul is limitless in what it can create. Your ability to go beyond your expectations of what you can achieve will be vast. Miracles will happen, bringing to you the energies necessary for your growth in all facets of your being. You will become expanded in feeling, thinking and doing. We can assist those of you who help yourselves. We are your backstage helpers, remember, while you are on centre stage. As you direct your play and perform your role with awareness and understanding of your true reason for being, we assist you from behind the scenes. Your truth of being will be revealed to the audience, who can then decide to learn from your role and take your messages and wisdom of all-knowing upon themselves.

Can you live as you feel in your heart and not as you think in your head? Can you live your truth each moment of each day knowing you need to be strong when disbelievers begin to question your way of being and knowing? We say to you this is your biggest test – the test of affirming the role you are playing to bring it to full fruition, with glory and honour for a job well done.

Many Ways to See the Truth

Each of you has your own perception of truth. As you live your own truth, you begin to understand that other people may have a different truth to yours and are also living truthfully as enlightened beings. Please understand you all are unique and living very different realities from each other. No one reality is the only or true reality. Whichever reality you are living is the true reality for you, and as you become aware of this you create the best possible reality available to you with the agenda you have set yourself in this particular lifetime.

When you are well on the way to being truthful to yourself and to those around you, much of your doubt about your agenda will go, and you will receive the confirmation you desire to give you courage to continue on your spiritual path.

Be aware that other people may not understand your perception of your truth, and may wish to criticise the way you are choosing to live your life. Please be strong and determined to live authentically, according to this wonderful truth of yours, with the knowledge that you have much support from Spirit. Only you know why you are in physical existence and what experiences you need to have.

Remember also that, as you stay strong and clear in your intentions, many new people will come into your life with new knowledge and opportunities for you. These are your new agents and actors in your play, to bring about the changes necessary for your advancement as a spiritual being. Those people no longer of assistance to you, or you for them, will move out of your life and go on their way as they will, meeting others who will be their agents. Please stay centred and loving as you live and speak your truth. Those who need to learn from you will see and hear what is necessary for their advancement.

Self Love

Love is a powerful emotion, and the most important emotion there is for humankind to experience. Without love, the human race would not survive. It is very important to have self-love, as without love for oneself one does not have love to give or share with others, be it another person, a plant, an animal or even the Earth. So many people have strong hate for others. This emotion is really one of fear, as fear is the opposite of love. As you learn to live in and with love for yourself, you have trust in your destiny. It unfolds as it is meant to do and all fear is gone.

When you no longer fear anyone or any situation, you truly become the very person you are meant to be. That is a truly authentic, positive energy that others will want to emulate. The nature of yourself is energy, and, if your energy is filled with love and trust, you have no room for fear to be part of you. Love energy is incredibly powerful in the way it can heal you and others with its touch and beauty.

You come to realise that your essence is pure energy manifested into the form you are at present. It is for a particular purpose, and your ability to transform your feelings of yourself into complete loving acceptance brings you the peace and joy every human is searching for. Loving yourself is the greatest step you can take toward your transformation.

Unconditional Love

When you love yourself unconditionally, with all your faults, you will have the ability to love others unconditionally. It is the most admirable trait you can have. Unconditional love for even the most unliked person you know reveals your ability to understand that all men and women are equal in the eyes of God/Goddess and universal wisdom.

Their reason for being as they are may not be apparent to you. This does not mean that you need to be their friend, or spend time in their space, but when you can respect their perspective and right to live as they choose, you expand your own power and wholeness.

Please consider that your ability to love unconditionally raises your levels of awareness. You have love for yourself, in awareness of your own vulnerability and imperfections. You are part of creation and have your particular role to play.

The person you find yourself giving unconditional love to may be the very one who assisted you at another time, in another life, when you needed it most. Even though they irritate you in this lifetime, it does not mean that they are not a soul mate. They may be in your life now specifically to provide you with an opportunity to learn about unconditional love. This is the very reason they are there for you.

As you love others unconditionally, remember to always love and respect yourself. By giving love unconditionally, we do not mean for you to give away your own power. You can be detached from the person receiving your love, and do not need to have a relationship with that person. You can give love from a distance, with the other person not knowing of your giving.

Loving Freely

To love unconditionally is the ultimate state of being, as you are then free to give respect to all humans no matter how they are treating you or living their lives. By having no expectations of them and no need to lean on them, you are free to give love openly and unreservedly, knowing you need nothing in return. This level of awareness and the giving of love to all, no matter what, bring you the love you require, even if it is from other sources. The energy you project will come back to you tenfold in every way imaginable, allowing you to live freely as you are meant to.

Loving freely opens your chakras to a lovely state of balance and harmony. It creates a perfect level of energy in which to achieve all that is necessary for completion of the tasks you have come here to do. The giving of love selectively, apart from in a romantic situation, hinders your progress and keeps you limited in your level of understanding.

Most people find that to give love freely is an extremely difficult challenge, as they are still bound up in their hurts and wounds from past experiences. They wish to protect themselves from being hurt again, so retract their natural instincts to give generously to others until they are confident of their intentions. We say, be discerning with strangers and those who are not open with you. Love, however, can be given in thoughts from a distance, and the receiver need not even know of this.

What is important is to think love, not hate. When you can eliminate hate from your feelings and thoughts, you will be well on the way to loving freely.

Fear of Loving

Watching from spirit, we observe that many humans live in total isolation. Their fear of loving themselves or others is so very strong that they are fearful of rejection and do not reach out to others for support. They do not trust their own self-love. We are concerned for you who live without the rewards of a loving companion, be it another adult, an animal or children.

Perhaps fear of not being approved of, or accepted as one is, is so strong you put up brick walls or create a personality that is intimidating, arrogant or aloof to protect yourself from yourself. Only when fear is removed can you find love and joy in your life. The way to remove this fear is to understand the reason for your being and the circumstances you are in.

Once again, it is awareness of who you truly are and the reason you are on this planet that brings you to a fulfilling, joyful, loving way of living. As you comprehend that you are a being of pure energy with a personality created to deal with the experiences you need to have, you can transform into a loving person. You can then begin to share your love energy with others, bringing them love from you, and many will be attracted to your beautiful energies.

Conditional Love

The love we call conditional is the love most humans think they desire the most, and is the most evasive of loves. Loving unconditionally is so much easier than loving conditionally. By this conditional love we mean the romantic kind, which humans are forever striving to have or find in a companion to walk with them on their journey through life. The reason for this desire is usually to bring to completion a search for wholeness. You do not realise that the only way to wholeness is within oneself – on finding your own wholeness you can then find your perfect partner.

Conditional love is the love one has when conditions for a relationship are suitable, and it enhances the wholeness of the people in relationship. We are very relieved when couples understand that they can retain their own identity within a relationship, preserving their own power base. This power base is your soul. When respect is given to each individual's right to be who they truly are, the conditions are right for a truly beautiful union.

The union of two beautiful souls, each living in their own power, is the pinnacle of man's greatest triumph for achievement in every way. The majority of people settle for second best, continuously living out their lives with unsuitable partners to whom they surrender their power, or living without understanding who they themselves truly are. Their lives are therefore not lived fully, and they forfeit the opportunity to live in great joy with someone who can enhance their wholeness, sharing the real meaning of their souls and their reason for being.

Denial of Love

When you were brought into this world, you came with love and loving intentions ingrained in your soul. You had expectations of living in a state of lovingkindness and loving experiences for the entire length of your lifetime. Some of you have been fortunate to continue to have and to fulfil these expectations, as you have lived in loving environments with much good fortune. Many of you, however, have found from early on that life is difficult, with unhappy and unloving experiences and conditions. You have felt unloved and unworthy of giving or receiving love.

The attitude you have developed and adopted may be of denial of giving or accepting love, because of a lack of self-worth. Denial is a way of not seeing the truth, or not facing up to what needs attention. If you deny the existence of some situation, or deny that anything is lacking, you think you do not need to address it.

This is a very sad state of being, as love is what is most important for mankind's evolution. With love, all things are possible.

By admitting to yourself first and foremost that you want to be loved, and deserve to be loved, you open up opportunities awaiting you. Yes, you may have had a terrible childhood, when nobody loved you, but this does not make you unlovable. Each person is unique and perfect in his or her imperfections, and you choose your experiences in which to learn. Do not deny yourself the wonderful experience of love. To begin with, give love out to others, even when you are feeling low and without self-love. Love will grow as you receive pleasure in the giving of it.

You will not need to wait long before loving energy returns to you in many ways. As you unlock the doors of your heart, you open up the floodgates so that you can experience all facets of love. You will see the wonder of the world with fresh eyes, be it in nature or with people.

The Way You Think

Thinking thoughts is a very powerful tool you have been given to create your desired reality. Your thinking is creator of your conscious actions and your reactions to other people's actions. We suggest that you spend time pondering on the quality of your thinking. Your thoughts create how you live your life: if your thoughts are positive, kind and loving you create a life of happiness and joy.

Wisdom develops while using your thoughts to create the best outcome in every situation. Thinking creatively and with consideration for all involved, you will find yourself creating a world of success and harmony, both for yourself and for those close to you.

If you feel your thoughts are not as positive and kind as you would like them to be, train yourself to think only beautiful, loving thoughts of the wonder of every person and situation, knowing that all is as it is for reasons perhaps unknown to you.

By projecting positive energies toward the focus of your attention, wise actions will result. You are a powerful being, and every thought you have is projected into producing a consequence somewhere. You are the cumulation of all you have thought until this particular moment in linear time.

Please ask the universe to help you have clarity of thought, with the intention of becoming the purest form of energy you have the potential to be. You are part of universal energy, and the more you think with positive, loving and creative thoughts, the more the universe will respond in this way. Those who do not think creatively and lovingly fall into the group of human beings who control and manipulate, or are easily controlled and manipulated, by negative energies. Think love and love your thinking!

The Beauty of
Your Thoughts

Beauty of action and thoughts brings you to a state of wholeness and purity. We consider that, as you let go of your past and move into the present moment, you have no further need for negative thoughts or actions. Thinking beautiful thoughts creates for you the powerful, positive future you desire. You send out to the universe affirming and giving messages, and these energies will be returned to you with beautiful, affirming people and situations that come into your life.

You are as you think. Quality thoughts result in quality events and creations in your life. Your thoughts can only be beautiful if your heart and emotions are healed and you love continuously. The ability to have gratitude for all your experiences, no matter how difficult, allows your heart to remain open to loving and to receiving love.

Thinking beautiful thoughts brings you yourself to a state of beauty. Others see you as a glowing example of magnificent energy that they will wish to emulate. Your aura is full of bright, clear colour, pulsating at high frequencies of love and light and drawing beauty and loving energy of like-minded people and matter to you.

Can you see how powerful your thoughts are in creating your future? Your projections come back to you and, in thinking with the clearest, purest intentions, your rewards will come. We consider that saying beautiful affirmations to your guides and angels on a daily basis will confirm your desires and intentions.

Please be disciplined in this way, and before long you will always think beautiful thoughts.

Coming of Angels
to Assist You

Your guides are with you, and you can have a lovely connection with them as you open up your trust and intuition. You also have the opportunity to connect with angels of many types. These beautiful energies can be accessed when you are in need of extra direction to follow your purpose in the physical realms.

With love, trust and openness, the angels come to you from afar with blessings, pouring in pure energy filled with love. Your connection with the angels is a beautiful experience for you, bringing you into a state of serene joy and contentment. Angels work with you on many levels, altering your vibrations and your attitudes to ideas and beliefs that need to be let go of, and creating room for new ideas and thoughts.

The Angel of Mercy will visit you when you are in need of balance and harmony. She works with your guides, assisting them to bring healing and renewal to you within your auric field.

The Angel of Relationships is always busy working to bring people together for growth, when the meeting of another person can enrich them.

The angels bring about much in the physical world by working behind the scenes. Their ability to manifest miracles is beautifully apparent when it does occur. Do you remember a time when events happened magically for you, with everything falling into place like a dream? Much is being orchestrated by the angels to bring about these possibilities.

Please be alert for magical happenings. With new understanding and alertness, more and more often these situations will occur for you. Any gratitude you give to the angels is most welcome, and always remember: angels are lovingly everywhere, willingly giving when asked.

Your Own Special Angel

You have a unique role on the Earth plane and you have assigned to you a special angel to assist with your purpose. You have your guides, who assist with day-to-day issues and actions, and a personal, overseeing angel. She/he is assigned to watch over you and guard you from inappropriate negative energies.

You will know of stories of people who have miraculously escaped a plane crash or drowning, for example. They may be the only one to survive, often completely unharmed. Their angel protected them, as it was not their time to leave the physical plane. Their survival brought to them a dramatic change in their perceptions and understanding of life. Usually this survivor is then available to assist many others with 'near death' experiences.

Angels have a different vibrational frequency field from you or your guides. It is of a different nature, and they are able to appear in many guises and in many places simultaneously, which perplexes those of you who are aware of their existence.

Your angel is with you now as you read and is lovingly waiting for you to communicate with them in your new awareness. Gratitude and recognition of their role in helping you will bring you a feeling of joy, wonder and trust. It allows events to unfold for you in the best possible way.

If you so desire, give your angel a name and speak with her/him each day, as well as with your guides, whom you may also name. By listening to your heart in the silence, a name will come to you: your angel will place it there. This name has the vibrational sound suitable for your angel. And drawing your angel on paper will be a lovely confirmation of your special connection.

Devas

Now that you know your own personal angel is with you, we can tell you of the angels who protect the environment. We call these angels devas. Their role is to work with nature to assist in keeping and restoring harmony and balance to the Earth, the environment where you live and play.

Mankind has not understood the fragility of Earth, and over many, many years has taken without respect or gratitude. Now is a very critical time: because of the destruction, the environment is drastically out of balance. The devas are available to repair the damage; however, they operate only as directed by mankind, when awareness is opened to the need for healing and love of the planet.

Much can be achieved swiftly when people lift their awareness and begin to put attention and loving energy into a desire for a better environment. All that is needed is to ask for assistance from the devic kingdom. With joint cooperation the desired healing can take place; for example clearing of polluted air in certain areas will be achieved when specific directions are given to the devas to assist. The intention must be clearly stated and the request made to the devas. The problem will be solved as if by magic.

You can achieve so much with cooperation from other realms, as you wake up to the understanding that you are not alone on planet Earth. Behind the scenes is a 'cast of thousands'. With clear directions from those of you on centre stage, their work will flow smoothly. Remember that you are both directing and playing a role in the play called life. The more you cooperate with the audience and backstage crew, the more successful will be your play.

Beauty in All You Experience

As your perception of your reality changes to one of love for all people and things, your eyes begin to see the beauty in all forms and actions. The world around you is magnificent, as the creation of the smallest insect to the largest tree is perfect in all ways. The wonders of nature are astoundingly beautiful, and man need only open his eyes to see this beauty in all there is around him. You are part of this beauty, and, in acknowledgment of and with respect for the manifestation of every living thing that co-exists with you, much loving energy can be exchanged in your moments of awareness.

Mankind has dominated nature, taking without loving respect for and without awareness of the importance and significance of the roles of the plants, animals and minerals, the oceans, wind, sun etc.

With awareness, you can perceive how wonderful it is to see a glorious sunset, or the reflection of the white clouds in a still pond, and take into yourself the love and joy of the feelings of that moment. This feeling sustains you when you are feeling sad or alone.

As you become more alert to the beauty of life, you see beauty in people's faces. You see the beauty in their smile and the kindness in their eyes. You notice the beauty in kind actions, no matter how insignificant these actions are. Beauty means different things to different people, and no two people have exactly the same reaction to, or sense of, beauty.

Energy is unique in its message for each soul. You create your own beautiful waves of energy with your thoughts of love and kindness; others receive these signals in their own unique way. Please continue to create your own beauty in all you do and say. Living in beautiful surroundings, no matter how humble, lovingly gives you perfect vibrations to live in.

The Sounds of the Angels

As you use your eyes to view the beauty of existence, so too can you use your ears to hear the beauty of all that is, through sound.

You enhance your transformation as you choose to listen to beautiful music whenever possible. With wonderful tones and rhythms, you bring your body and soul into perfect vibration, resonating in harmony with all that is the purest in sound and of the highest.

The music you select needs to be of pure resonance and pitch, and in its selection you nourish your soul with tones of the angelic realms. All beautiful music has its origin in the essence of angels. They bring forth the inspirational sounds that reach the composers of your music, so that your ears and feelings recognise those patterns of resonance that heal and soothe.

Whenever possible, fill your homes and places of work with these angelic sounds. They keep your frequencies high and in harmony, allowing you to live your truth so much more radiantly. The soothing sounds assist you and all with you to feel joyful and at peace with your intentions in that space you have created. The rhythms and tones you hear and feel help in your healing and upliftment in all you are focusing on in that moment.

The selection of only harmonious music is very important for your soul, there being many variations of beat and tone that are suitable.

For example the sound of drums resonates deeply into your cells, reminding you of your tribal connections. Enjoy moving to these beats. Dancing to music releases you to express your deepest feelings. The more you dance, the more you integrate your body with your soul.

Of course the sounds of nature, such as the breeze rustling through the trees, waves breaking on a shoreline and birdsong, are nature's natural harmonies to bring you the beauty of all that is. Listen and enjoy!

The Way to Happiness

Please consider the times when you are at your happiest. Is it when you are being given, or giving, expensive gifts or having an expensive experience? Do you have a wonderful new dress or suit that makes you happy? Or is it that a nagging inside you – a little voice – says that it is wonderful to have these things and you are meant to feel happy, but the emptiness is still there? Happiness does not come from acquiring material possessions – having a new flash car or the best house in the street.

Happiness is held within the smallest gesture given to you with kind and loving thoughts by someone, which helps you to glow with warmth inside. It is the sharing of a moment with someone you love – watching a beautiful sunset or experiencing a shared moment of laughter over the understanding of a funny situation you are in together. Happiness is the contentment that comes when you feel complete within yourself, accepting your so-called faults and loving yourself totally as you are.

You know that you are a unique part of the universe with under-standing that everything is as it is meant to be for you. God gives overwhelming love to you continuously and unconditionally. You have no need to possess things for security or happiness, as your wealth is within you. It is the quality of your thinking, feeling and being that brings you all you have ever dreamt of having and more.

We consider that, as you simplify your needs and desires for material possessions, your happiness will increase accordingly. You free yourself from all those trappings that have bound you to your past conditioning. As you free yourself, much of your thinking is simpler and clearer, and your truth shines forth brightly.

Love or Fear –
the Choice Is Yours

The human race has always possessed free will. We ask you now to live positively in love, and with love. There is no joy in living negatively and finding fault with much in your reality. Those of you who are living positively understand that the very essence of your being is love, and as you live with loving intent you attract to you a loving, positive nature in the form of happenings, people and possessions.

Those of you who live negatively are full of fear and cannot trust your own ability to create a future that is full of lovely events and people. Fear is a wasteful energy that brings the very events most feared to those living with it: manifestation occurs as a result of these fearful thoughts. You attract to you that which you create in your own thoughts.

When you live positively with love, that which you give out returns to you: you create your own reality. Those whose reality is of the highest thought and action receive back energy of this calibre. We say to those of you who live with fear of any kind – please let go of that fear, whether it be of dying, sickness or lack of love, money or success.

Remember you are a spiritual being having a human experience, and all that is happening in your life for you is part of your experience – part of your play. As you detach from issues and worries at hand, and their outcomes, you can begin to observe the reasons behind these issues. You can let go of all attachment and any fears you may have, trusting that all will be well.

Living in love and with love, you shut out negative energy and in doing so you eliminate the opportunity for anything negative reaching you. The stronger your love energy, the weaker is your negative energy, and soon your whole being radiates a strong, loving energy field and all fear dissipates from around you.

Many Facets of
Yourself Within

We have talked about the helpers and advisers who are all around you, both in your physical reality and in Spirit. Now we wish to explain to you more about yourself. You know now about your soul, the real you. Your personality is the identity you are presenting to the world in this lifetime.

At different times, with different situations, people or moods, you present a certain persona to people. You may be the serious, disciplined scholar or the frivolous, irresponsible playgirl or playboy. Within each of you lie many individual layers or facets and, as the circumstances change, so you bring to the surface the most appropriate expression of yourself to meet the demands made of you. It is very healthy to express all parts of yourself.

You are multidimensional and multifaceted, and your soul encompasses this very easily. In fact your soul wishes to encourage you to show all sides of your authentic self, within the framework of love, kindness and sincerity. For example many people have a creative side for art, dance, singing or gardening, and do not take the opportunity to grow using their abilities in this way.

Other facets of yourself that you may not be using are your ability to organise, write or speak out your truth. You have many hidden talents and abilities yet unexpressed. To become a complete human, we encourage you to explore these new areas, stretching yourself in ways you have not considered until now.

Now, with your new understanding of the very wonderful support you have behind the scenes, you can trust yourself to explore these new options. Many of your guides are experts in one particular facet of you that you have not expressed. There will be one guide who specialises in creativity, one for logical matters and so on, so please ask for the guide most appropriate for the task in hand.

Please do not forget to have fun. There will always be many willing guides to assist you to do that.

Living in Multidimensional Reality

Living as a three-dimensional being has given you many very important physical experiences. As you have chosen to be in a physical body, this is very much part of your growing as a spiritual being. Now, as you master physical reality, learning issues of major importance, you can move more into your many other areas of being, those that you have neglected or blocked out from your daily life.

The very nature of you is to be telepathic and intuitive, and now is the time for you to utilise these abilities as a normal part of your life. As you become more intuitive, you will no longer rely on others to assist you in making decisions. You will just know what you need to do or say, as your intuition will be unlocked from your heart and free to guide you at all times.

As you live using your intuition constantly, you connect with others who are also doing the same. This then allows you to telepathically communicate with them on an ongoing basis, and you have no need to speak with them verbally to convey your thoughts and feelings.

This is also possible with friends and family who are physically far away. All you need do is think of them from your heart, and they will receive your message. Please enjoy this new ability and use it for loving and caring intentions. We suggest you practise with your loved ones and wait for confirmation from them of the message you sent their way.

Many other abilities will be available to you also, such as teleporting and astral travel, not only in your sleeping state but also consciously by declaring your intentions. We are very aware that many of you are already able to achieve these states of existing, and know how exhilarating it is for you to explore them.

Experiencing
Other Dimensions

As you transform to live a new kind of existence, your ability to move between many dimensions will occur. Your vibrations alter, depending in which dimension you wish to be, and much of your time will be spent in more fascinating realms than your physical reality. This happens very easily for you as your awareness awakens. You will transcend smoothly to these other states of being.

Much of your existence will be in what we call mystical, dreaming states, with your physical body at rest as in meditation. At times you can have parts of yourself unconsciously elsewhere, as you perform routine tasks. This ability allows you to experience the many creative processes of your feelings, by actually playing other roles that are important to your psyche in other dimensions.

It is similar to watching a movie, only you will be in the movie, experiencing what it feels like to be playing the part you are in. You will find your growth accelerates in all ways, with this ability to know how it feels to be betrayed, loved, rejected and so on in the many situations you will find yourself in.

As you have these experiences presented to you, you bring to your physical reality a new depth of understanding for those around you.

Much of your physical time can then be spent assisting those in need of support, using encounters you yourself have experienced. Empathy for others is then so much easier for you, as you have felt the very emotions they are feeling in their physical life.

The wisdom and knowing of your being are once again activated to their full potential, and your purpose is at last very clear to you.

Soul Mates

Living as a physical being does not preclude you from continuing your relationships with those from your own spiritual realms. As a spiritual being, you have achieved certain levels of understanding and intelligence, depending on the growth you have experienced during your existence.

You share similar energy patterns and frequencies to others from your many realms of existence. At times these similar energies stay with you in spirit, as you undertake your experience in the physical world. They may be your guides and advisers behind the scenes. Some manifest as other humans on the Earth and are with you on your journey through this present life.

Many of you call these people soul mates, as you have a knowing of who they really are and a knowing of a profound connection with them. They are from your soul clan, having the same energy frequency. When you meet one of your soul mates you have an instant rapport and feel very comfortable with them.

Some of these soul mates have come into your life to help you learn very important lessons through the experiences that you have with them. Not all of these experiences are joyful ones. Please remember, they are agents for your spiritual growth and, no matter how disastrous or unwelcome the experience, it is as planned for you. Be grateful to them and acknowledge the part they have played in bringing you further along your spiritual path; then let go of them and move on.

One or more soul mates may be assigned to you to be your partner in this lifetime, as a companion and often as a romantically faceted dimension for sexual expression and the raising of children together. The nature of your being is to have a partner, so please wait for this soul mate to arrive, as they will. Please do not compromise with someone who is not of your energy frequency.

Your soul knows.

Being Your Own Church

Now that you have found that your God does not need to be worshipped in a church, as you have always known it to be, you can be your own church. You can visit your church every minute of every day. You do not need to put money in the collection tray or listen to other people's truths. You can listen to your own truth, by listening to the very core of your being. This is not difficult when you have practised listening to your heart and gained wisdom in this way. With meditation in all its forms you can go deep within yourself and connect with the very purest, loveliest centre of yourself. This brings you to a state of God consciousness, and as you reach this state your world changes to a new reality. You bring into play all the facets of yourself that were mentioned earlier, in their most energetic form and in total harmony. You begin to vibrate at high frequencies, and your attunement to all dimensions of yourself takes place.

You understand that you have easy access to all the libraries of knowledge in the universe. This is the very best way for you to remember all you have forgotten of who you truly are and why you are here. Other churches cannot tell you this, so why go on being involved in other people's truths? We believe you gain your own strength and freedom when you visit your God/Goddess within your very own church. This is all you need to create the very best possible circumstances for yourself and to fulfil your role in this lifetime.

The nature of your existence is a unique part of creation. Know your uniqueness – you walk your own journey. The greatest journey you can take in this lifetime is the one within yourself.

Your church is your body, and your soul awaits your visit – as often as you choose. The soul resides within and is connected with God – all creation is one. Peace and joy await you.

Part Two

Assisting Others to Transform

This second part of this book is for those of you who have transformed into a wonderful being of light, constantly thinking loving thoughts and using your intuition. Live your life in the very best way possible and assist others to transform into their highest possible being. We are delighted as more and more of you become truly beautiful humans emanating love and joy in your life.

Many of you may find it difficult to live in truth, using your best intentions as you juggle a very demanding job and interact with others who are not as aware or awake as you. Please treat yourself gently and have the courage to stand firm with your new understanding of your reason for being. Gradually you will feel more comfortable in your so-called alien surroundings.

Your frequencies and vibrations are much higher and faster than are those of the ones who are not transformed, and, even though you may have difficulty adjusting to their energies, they will certainly feel good when they are touching yours. In your higher level of being, your energies are protected and continuously nurtured using the universal energy that pours into your energy field on an ongoing basis, as you ask for it. We suggest you meditate every day to recharge, using this source of nourishment, and you will know that you are continually maintaining your connection with the divine source of all energy.

The following pages provide assistance in ways you can best use your abilities with all you meet in your day-to-day life.

As you read on, you will see that your reason for being is to be spiritually aware and to use this awareness to serve and assist others in their own paths to transformation.

Power Within

Energy provides power, and you are all made of energy. The nature of you is as an energy vibration and, as you purify your energy and raise it to the very highest level available for you this lifetime, you have the greatest source of power. Not only is your power for your own advancement, it is to be available for healing and guiding many people.

Power is the word we use for manifesting all you desire. When you are self-empowered, you can create miracles for yourself and others with much ease and little effort. You only need to tap into this power to bring into your life the events and experiences necessary for achieving your agenda, your purpose.

We understand your need for experiences of many types and can manifest events that are perfect learning situations for your growth. Living in and with your own power source enables you to resolve these experiences with the very best outcomes. The outcome will always be advantageous to your soul.

In tapping into your own internal power, you find that your solutions bring you closer to God/Goddess and the divine knowing you had forgotten. When you continuously seek assistance from other people, you lose your power, giving it away to those you seek the help from. Many a time, however, asking for guidance is very sensible.

But, ultimately, all your decisions are best made by using your intuition – listening to your heart and not your head.

As you gain confidence in the decisions you make, your power within grows and you blossom naturally and beautifully as who you truly are. The power of each individual is immense, and as you all become selfempowered the need for assistance from government agencies and welfare will lessen. Many people who now rely on handouts from these agencies are very weak and have given away their power. If only they could understand that they are themselves very powerful beings.

We encourage you to turn on your power within.

Staying Detached from Other People's Dramas

Detachment is the opposite of attachment. Most humans are very attached to people and things in their lives. They are also very attached to their values and habits, finding it difficult to look at other ways of thinking and living.

People are attached to their way of living and find themselves becoming immersed in friends and/or relations' lives and problems. They do not understand the significance of the dramas being created around them. They are often created to give these other people power, or to pull in sympathy in a victim sort of way.

As you come to understand this, you can detach from the dramas of others. Be a helping friend without giving away your power or energy to them. Become alert and aware of your own power and wholeness, and see with greater clarity the issues being played out. Unless you are directly involved in the drama yourself, stay detached. This is the best position from which to assist, as you will not give away your soul. In this way you can be in your own power and give advice from a distance, just as your guides assist you when appropriate.

Loving detachment becomes a position in which you can move on with your own issues. When you are detached from your own dramas, you see them more clearly and choose actions that are wise and which offer you and others concerned the best possible outcomes. At times you will be called upon to state your view on issues or happenings around you, be they local or global. In such instances non-identification with the issue will assist you to remain in your truth and power, and not identify with fear or conflict. This will keep you free, with your energy intact to retain your wholeness and focus only on truth.

The Wonder of Nature

As you are at one with the universe, you are at one with nature. All living things are one with you. You are all made of the same matter and, as your awareness of this grows, you discover that you can communicate with all of nature as you do with your guides. All components of nature resonate at their own frequency levels. Your own frequency level also varies, depending on your level of awareness and wakefulness.

When you are at a high frequency of vibration, you can begin to communicate with the animals, trees and plants, rocks, rivers, oceans etc. Understand that each part of nature has its own particular role in the scheme of things and, as you give recognition and respect to each beautiful part, your energies blend. An exchange of love and comfort for mutual benefit takes place. Dramatic changes can take place in you, the plants, animals and water, for example, when you give loving attention to them.

Those of you with gardens notice that plants thrive when you talk to them. This is more important than fertiliser and water, although they are also very necessary for survival. You create for them wonderful conditions for fulfilling their highest potential. With love, nature is in harmony with you and assists you to reach your highest potential also.

Spend as much time as you can in nature and, as you do, perceive the plants and animals, and the sand or grass you may be sitting on, as one with you. Give gratitude to them for being as they are, and ask for assistance to bring you into a high level of awareness with them. Give love and healing to all of nature, and ask also to be shown how you can assist them to live in their highest level of potential. Remember you and nature are one, intertwined with each other during your journey through existence on Earth.

Communicating with Nature

Being one with nature brings you to an understanding of the vastness of creation. The beginning of existence brought to the planet Earth many simple forms of life that began the chain of events and conditions creating the ecological structure suitable for bringing human beings onto the scene. As man has evolved to the level he is at today, he has relied on the plants and animals around him to supply his food, shelter and comfort.

The early humans understood the nature of their surroundings, but most of mankind today has lost this understanding. Most people live separately from nature and do not consider it as a vital part of their lives. Much of human disease is the result of man's lack of oneness with nature, even though it offers wonderful support and love to all who are awake and aware of this vital role.

As you return your perceptions to merging into oneness with nature, you learn of mutual support while you listen to the messages continually being given to you from the plants, animals and elements. As you hug a tree, listen to it. It is speaking for all trees: this one tree is connected to all trees. The message may be for you to stand up and speak your truth regarding the diminishing rainforests throughout the world. It may be to tell you to plant more trees in your neighbourhood, or simply to give you love and comfort when you need it most for your own personal issues.

As you listen to the wind it may be telling you to move house, as the winds of change are beginning to blow for you in your purpose of being. Animals, including birds, may visit you to affirm trust in the choices that you have made. They are always coming with messages of confirmation, and work with us to heal and restore faith when times are difficult.

The understanding of these synchronistic happenings assists you in living with trust and courage for your life purpose. Remember, answers to your questions are there for you right before your eyes in nature.

Creation and Living in This Present Reality

This reality you live in now is only one of many, many you have lived in and even are living in at this moment in time. By this we mean that you can be having many realities in many different dimensions, all interconnecting. You have chosen to be in this reality of yours now, in your time and space. In actuality, time and space are very human/ Earth measurements. Beyond, all things are possible. Know that so much is possible beyond your realms of understanding. As you grow in awareness, you can break free of many limiting factors and narrow boundaries of thinking that have been shown to you in this life. You develop the ability to know of all that is outside mankind's inhibited library of knowledge of creation.

The planet Earth is only one small part of the infinity of creation. The human race on planet Earth is one of many, many civilisations existing in all of creation. Perhaps you have not been very success- ful in the way you have looked after and respected your home, over a long inhabitation. Perhaps, as more and more of you wake up to this understanding, you will be able to redress the balance, restoring Earth to a place of beauty and serenity where love is the energy most noticeable and respected.

You in the human form are a reflection of your home and, as you evolve to new ways of being in body and spirit, so will the Earth. She is changing rapidly, just as you are changing rapidly; harmony is required within you as much as outside of you to achieve a perfect progression. Creation has set the agenda for this to happen, with cooperation between all concerned. Please assist so that this can be achieved.

Living in the Now

Living in the now is the essence of existing in the moment. You are energy, and your energy needs to be fully active in every moment of your being. As you live fully in each moment with authentic intention, you create for yourself the very best possible future.

As you live radiantly in each moment, you send out messages with high-quality potential. This enables you to connect with other energies of high-quality potential. Merging with other beautiful energies, you create for yourself a wonderful magnetic force and attract to you all you desire and deserve. You achieve this with intentions and actions that are full of love and caring. Energy is wasted when your thoughts are in the past or too far into the future. By placing your attention there, you are not focused on the crucial area of your existence – now, which is all you really have. You miss the opportunities and messages being given to you from Spirit if you neglect each moment of the present, now. As you act on your opportunities, your experiences are lived with the best possible potential.

Awareness and alertness to the moment in hand create your true pathway on your amazing journey in this lifetime. You can see with clarity and vision, knowing your attention is on every moment as it happens. We suggest you trust that the future will take care of itself as you live each moment to full capacity and with loving intent.

The Nature of You
as a Vital Being

As a vital being, you can achieve all you wish to achieve by living in your own power within. Being vital allows you to access your wisdom from many, many lifetimes. In accessing this wisdom you can be completely in charge of this life of yours now.

You are not swayed by falsehoods or tempted to make ill-conceived and wrong choices. You have a knowing of how you are best suited to live and behave. You make the wisest choices, even when faced with a so-called easy solution to a problem.

Living with great vitality and passion for life creates the opportunities for you to further your spiritual evolution, by whatever means you have chosen in this lifetime. Your knowingness of who you truly are guides you to the opportunities and experiences you need. By being fully alert to your experiences and why they are there for you, your choices of resolution within these experiences are the very wisest you can make. As you become aware of your own soul and the reasons for your return to Earth, you can use your great vitality, passion and wisdom to open up the vitality of many others who come into your life.

The nature of your vitality is your oneness with God/Goddess within. Your beautiful alignment with the creative force allows you to live your life fully and with awareness that you are in charge of your reason for being, and all others are actors in your play of life. You need not allow any of them to control your thinking, feeling or actions.

You are the master of your own destiny.

Being Enlightened

Light is at the very centre of you. Energy creates light, and light can bring you to the source of all knowingness. Many of you may ask: Which light is it that you mean? Light as the opposite of darkness or light as opposite of heavy? We mean both: your light is both showing you the way and taking away heavy burdens. As you move into the light inside you, you become more aware of who you truly are and are more enlightened to your reason for being. You can then cast off many of your old habits, possessions and even people that no longer have value in your life.

Not only will you have new perceptions of your own reality, you will understand that you have many realities in which you live at the one time. There is much merriment as you explore your many options of living in the light. You can uplift your energies and frequencies to such heights as darkness and heaviness go out of your life and you begin to live as an enlightened soul.

A connection with God/Goddess, the source of all creation, manifests for you an ability to be harmonious with all you touch and do in your reality. By this we mean you walk your journey with joy, grace and much success, and spread these attributes to all you meet. The light of your life shines brightly for others to follow and, as your light shines out with clarity, comfort and steadfastness, those who have been confused will perhaps begin to seek solace in spending time in your light.

Enlightenment may be only the beginning of your journey to know yourself, as up till now your journey has been to find and remember your true self. You are one with God/Goddess, and the knowing of your true self means the knowing of God/Goddess. God consciousness brings you to the state we call enlightenment, and then you can proceed to know and live as an embodiment of God in the physical form. With this realisation comes your true fulfilment as a human being. This is your reason for being.

The Best Way to
Live Your Life

Being an enlightened being in this lifetime of yours now is the best opportunity for you as a soul to assist the human race to evolve into new ways of living. With awareness and wisdom of the nature of existence, you can share this great knowledge of yours with others. The sharing of your wisdom can only be achieved when the person you are with is willing to learn and to observe how you conduct your life. Those who are not willing, or are totally unaware of other ways of being, cannot be helped. Only those who are ready are open to receive and learn from you. The opportunities are there for you to facilitate growth in others by your example and, in facilitating them, to joyously experience their own understanding and truth. The facilitating we mean for you to do is that of creating situations and opportunities by which those who wish to can move forward in their own spiritual growth.

We suggest that you speak your own truth as often as possible when the opportunity arises. Live your life as you truly know it, enjoying a spiritual experience in the physical form, with all the understanding this encompasses.

The need for material possessions will begin to diminish, as will the worry of making money to reserve for a retirement you will not have. You become contented, with all you desire to keep you stimulated and limitless in the way you live each day. Manifestation of all you need is presented to you as you live with loving intent and a willingness to serve and give of your wisdom and energy to those who are ready to listen and learn.

The very nature of your being is to be a beacon of light for others. As you truly embrace your existence as a representative of God/Goddess and all creation, you will truly be living as you are meant to.

Your New Existence
with Others

As a transformed being of light who has much awareness and understanding of your reason for being in the physical form, you will begin to notice how differently you feel when you are with those who have not begun their spiritual journeys. You will find that you are uncomfortable in this, as we might say, alien company. We suggest that you need to prepare yourself each time you go out your front door or have visitors who you know will not have your level of understanding. This preparation need only take a few moments and it is in your thinking. And as you think, so you shall be.

We want you to think of yourself as having a beautiful ball of light surrounding you. This ball of light can be any colour you wish, only make it a clear, bright happy colour. You will be protected from people's lesser vibrations in this ball. Your own high and rapid vibrations still reach out to those you come into contact with so that they will continue to benefit from being in your auric field, but you will not be drained of your energy. You will dramatically affect the auric field of others in a positive way.

This is a most important ritual for you to do each day as you move your vibrations up to high levels. You will find that many people will want to be near you and with you often. They recognise in you a state of being that they wish to have. You will find, as you begin to feel comfortable with yourself in these higher realms of existence, you can create magical happenings in your life and for those touched by your beautiful energy. You are made of energy, and the purer and lighter it is, the further it will spread in a loving and powerful way. Remember your new existence is in many dimensions of yourself, which allows you to access the knowledge of creation.

Colour Your Life

Live the life you live with all the colours of the rainbow, in every tone imaginable. These colours affect your emotions more than you realise, as their qualities have great impact on you in many ways. The vibrancy of colour in three-dimensional reality is very demure in comparison with that in the higher dimensions. Not only are the colours brighter and clearer, but there are many more shades and tones, which have the ability to create a stronger emotional reaction.

Each colour has the ability to heal and give love to certain aspects of you. You may find some days you favour wearing one colour and not another to feel comfortable and happy; another day you will find yourself more comfortable in a very different colour. Please notice your choices to determine if there is a correlation between how you are feeling and the colour you are wearing. Many of you may find the colours with which you decorate your homes are reflections of your personality type. As you begin to change and grow in your understanding of who you truly are, you may feel a need to change your colour scheme in your home as well as the colours you wear. We suggest it may be important for you to sometimes wear a colour you avoid, as this may be a colour associated with something lacking in your identity. By wearing it, you strengthen this so-called weakness in yourself. Become aware of all the colours of the rainbow and make a conscious effort to have some of each colour in your daily living somewhere.

You can choose a colour for each day of the week and wear something of that specific colour on that day. Be aware of everything you notice in this colour of your choice during the day – for example cars, the people you see wearing this colour and flowers. Perhaps meditate early in the day and state your intention of colour, relating it to its chakra. In this way you strengthen that part of your being in a very positive way.

Colour Your Thoughts

We mentioned earlier how important it is to think positively and creatively: your thoughts create your reality. Your thinking also affects those around you as the thoughts you have are picked up in the energy that is whirling around you, extending far beyond your auric field. You send the intentions of your thoughts out into the atmosphere and they become part of the collective thoughts of all mankind. As you think, so you are, and you bring to you what you have spent time thinking about.

We suggest you surround your thoughts with colours – the colours that hold the intentions for your desires. Each colour has a vibration and quality of its own. With your thoughts of love, think of the colour pink; strengthen your loving thoughts in conveying a prayer of hope and healing with the colour pink too. You will find that you assist others to heal using green and pink together. The energies will be taken to the person in need of healing and they will receive, not only your thoughts of love and healing, but also the energy in colour form. This is a very powerful and accurate way of assisting others to heal and move forward on their paths to transformation.

The vibrations contained in the colour you send in your thoughts penetrate deeply through the layers of the auric field and enter into the physical body of the needy person, with excellent results.

All you need do is sit in a quiet place, think of the person in need and give the directions, for example loving pink and healing green energy to be sent where required. Trust in the process is important, as are honour and authenticity in what you are doing. Other colours also bring miraculous results for those concerned when used appropriately; for example yellow, for vibrancy and mental achievement, can be sent to someone sitting an examination. Explore your ability to help others in this way.

Building Bridges
to the Future

Your transformation to a new way of existing brings the need for you to prepare to live differently, using your new abilities and awareness. You may no longer feel comfortable living as you have done and may need to move house, city or even country, to be in the very best vibrational location for what and who you now need to be.

We can assist you to build a bridge to take you there, leaving behind your old ways of being. This is not an easy task for you, as you have family and friends who have not yet been transformed. Be gentle on yourself and ease your way forward, in very slow steps. The bridge to your new life is built with trust in yourself and your ability to let go of old memories, values, habits and possessions. As you let go, give gratitude for the experiences and concepts you have learnt along your journey. Explain to those close to you that the changes are necessary for you to fulfil your reason for being. Give your explanations in a loving and thoughtful way and you will assist your loved ones to come to an understanding that perhaps they may want to change how they live their lives.

Trust and have courage, and the bridge to the new you will strengthen and become solid enough for you to walk on it. Your steps will no longer need to be tentative. You become more open in your thoughts and ideas, creating a path of excitement and curiosity as you move ahead. Explain your thinking as you move along, and give details to all who wish to know. Even the smallest thoughts, new ideas and ways of perceiving may open the eyes of those you least expected. As miracles happen for you, share and explain them to others. They too may then have the courage to take steps toward their transformation and journey across their own bridge towards an exciting future.

Compassion for Those You Assist

Assisting others in whatever way is the best for you, so that they may come to the understanding of a deeper meaning of life, will become your major purpose. Humans have chosen to be in physical form at this present time and to bring major changes to the evolutionary process of being human. As each of you wakes up to your memories of who you truly are, your major focus is in bringing others to this awareness. You are all at different levels of being, and your souls are also from many levels of existence, so we ask you to have understanding for those who are many grades or levels behind you in remembering their wisdom.

Compassion brings support for them as they struggle to let go of the need for security, material possessions and the narrow structure of their lives. With your insight into where they are at, you can give them the confidence to begin to take risks and branch away from the narrow, limited confines of how they live. Letting them know that they are worthwhile human beings – and loved – will give them the courage to explore further. With the knowing of your loving support they may take a tentative step to begin a new way of living.

Compassionate forgiveness for deeds of an unworthy nature done in the past are very necessary in the letting go of judgmental attitudes toward others. It enables souls to be free to explore the new. Your task is to reassure them and encourage them to move on, allowing the past to be forgiven and forgotten. Your task is to assist them to live in the present moment and to be alert to all the beautiful opportunities there are for them, trusting they are more than they believe themselves to be. You realise that you are no more than they: you are fortunate to have awakened earlier so that you can be of assistance in bringing others to the same lovely state of transformation as you are now experiencing. With great love, compassion and forgiveness, many miraculous events and opportunities come for all who are ready.

Letting Go of Expectations

Society presents you with many beliefs and expectations in how you are meant to live your life. You are encouraged to conform to society's expectations for behaviour and employment. You are expected to be conformist and to do what the law and governments expect of you. You are expected to go to school, university if possible, gain a good job, marry, have children, retire and then die! There is very little expectation for you to be creative, with independent thoughts, or have a different way of living.

Question this expectation and control of your way of being, and become a trailblazer with the courage to be different. Be courageous enough to step beyond the normal and not worry about what people think of you. Push the boundaries and stand up for what you know is the best way for you; you will break new ground for you and for others to follow. You may find others have had similar feelings and thoughts but have not had the courage to show their true colours.

By speaking out your truth and putting it into action, you set in motion the changes that are needed for new expectations of living. This helps you to change your own expectations for your personal life, and you will begin to see that the best way to live is with no set expectations but for the very best outcome for your highest good. By letting go of your old expectations, you allow a shift in perceptions that is necessary for a shift in being. Without this shift in perception, there can be no growth.

Trust that you are being guided to where you need to be in your reality for the work needing to be done. There is a big picture, and, with your willingness to surrender all preconceived ideas of how your life might be, we can direct you more easily. This does not mean you need not visualise your intentions and look forward into your future without plans. Please do so. Your real plans will, however, be in the deepest knowing in your heart, and will not come from expectations outside of you.

Being at Ease in
Your Own Reality

In transformation, freedom to be your authentic self is a relief. You can relax and let go of previous expectations of yours when you were exploring the mysteries of your reason for being. You will begin to live easily with this new you of light and love as you gain a much deeper understanding of your uniqueness and perfection. There are many shifts of perception and awareness in your transformational time.

During these shifts there may be awkwardness and you may feel uncertain of who you are becoming. With the final shift, however, a feeling of ease becomes normal. You and others adapt to who you are now; the time comes when you reflect back on whom you used to be and happily let go of that person and all associated with it. In becoming all you are here to be, burdens lift from your thoughts and feelings, creating a state of bliss and joy in all you are and do.

Remember your reality is created by you, with you being director and actor of your play for this lifetime. You create your own powerful intent to bring into play the very highest intentions, for your wellbeing. Make plans and create visions for the very best possible future.

Others are not to direct your play, even if they are actors in it. You live with free will, yet you are the director, creating necessary experiences with authenticity in every moment of your being. The other actors can feel at ease when they follow your directions and it is apparent there is loving intent and thoughtfulness in every action taken. Live with truth and bliss in all you do to be a role model for those who seek you out.

The Joy of Discovery of
What Lies Beyond

In conclusion, what lies beyond your present world of existence? We wish to explore this with you. You are transforming to a new existence. What is this new existence and why do you need to be transformed to a different way of being and thinking?

The world beyond today will be a perplexing one for those who have not made the shift in their vibrations that enables them to accommodate the changes in the Earth's vibrational frequencies. They are speeding up, and you also need to speed up yours to stay in tune with the Earth and to be able to resonate comfortably. This is a change in dimensions for you, so that you will have access to the fourth and fifth dimensions of being to live in, as well as the present third-dimensional reality. In these other dimensions of yourself you will discover your ability to connect with the spiritual realms, you will have access to knowledge of universal wisdom, you will be able to teleport, psychically heal others and use your telepathic skills with ease.

These abilities have always been available to the few who have been curious and explored spiritual realms, and to others who carried these abilities into this lifetime openly and did not suppress them.

The time is coming now for all humans to move forward into this state of awareness and to use these suppressed abilities openly. The time and conditions are now here for opening up and moving into new ways of living. This future is not to be feared, but welcomed with joy and excitement for the potential evolutionary growth of humankind. You are at the forefront of this new and amazing transformation of what it is to be human.

Open up your hearts and minds; trust the extraordinary changes now happening to you and your loved ones. Have courage and strength, as you trust the knowing that all will be well for you and the world.

In the stillness of my mind
Is the beauty of my heart;
In the stillness of my mind
I know I am not apart.
In the stillness of my mind
Lies the silent preparation,
As – in the stillness of my mind
Is the wonder of creation.

Merriene Scott

Merriene Scott welcomes
your correspondence.
Please contact her at

Email: merriene@merrienescott.com
www.merrienescott.com

www.ingramcontent.com/pod-product-compliance
Lightning Source LLC
Chambersburg PA
CBHW050948050726
47592CB00007B/2478